S T A R S
OVER LATIN AMERICA

STORY BY
M. EARL SMITH

ILLUSTRATIONS BY
GUSTAVO FERRÉS

MICHELKIN | PUBLISHING
ROSWELL, NEW MEXICO
BOOKS.MICHELKIN.COM

Other children's titles from Michelkin Publishing:

Adventures Through the Trees by Kay Gehring
Dear Sun, Dear Moon by Deborah Paggi & Gayle Cole
Wish Upon A Lantern by Lindy Lorenz & Beth Kruziki

ISBN: 0-9995222-4-8
ISBN-13: 978-0-9995222-4-0

DEDICATION

To all the peoples of Latin America, and to the dream of a united, socialist Americas.

I n Buenos Aires, there two young men, Ernesto and Alberto. Both were brilliant students, with Alberto studying biology and Ernesto studying medicine.

Their life was a good one, filled with plenty of time for leisure. They played sports, enjoyed their families, and lived a life that was, by the standards of the time, happy and comfortable.

However, each of them knew that there was more to the world, and their homeland of South America, than they knew.

One summer afternoon, as they lounged under a tree, Alberto turned to his friend and grinned.

"Che, we should take a trip across this continent of ours, and see everything there is to see before we settle down into our adult lives."

Che offered his friend a smile. "Alberto, that sounds delightful, but how are we going to do such a thing? Are we going to walk?"

"No!" Alberto exclaimed, "We're going to take The Mighty One!"

Che laughed. "Your motorcycle will not take us across South America, my friend!"

In spite of this, a decision was made: the two friends would take a year from their studies to experience the continent they called home.

A plan was made. On the back of The Mighty One, the pair would visit parts of their native Argentina, before traveling on to Chile, Peru, Colombia, and Venezuela.

The trip was not to be just for pleasure, however, as the pair both felt a strong desire to spend some time working at a leper colony in Peru.

When the day came, Che and Alberto loaded their supplies on the back of The Mighty One and said goodbye to their families.

Everyone smiled and waved, and winced a little when the pair was nearly hit by a bus!

Before they left Argentina, Che decided to make a detour to a local resort, so that he could see Chichina, his beloved.

They were only supposed to stay for two days, but the lovesick Che managed to stretch the visit for more than a week!

Finally, at Alberto's insistence, the pair left. Chichina gave him gifts before their departure, including a bracelet and fifteen American dollars.

The first part of the journey was rough. While in Argentina, the pair experienced several problems, including...

...a breakdown of The Mighty One, which led to an accident...

...that left the pair caught in a storm, which...

...blew away their tent, which forced them to...

...take shelter in a barn owned by a rich rancher who...

...forced them to leave on the back of a half-broken motorbike into a snowstorm in the Andes Mountains!

Despite some early troubles, the pair soon reached Chile, the "Backbone of South America."

It was here that they met a local reporter who wrote a story about their journey and the volunteer work they had planned for Peru.

Soon, The Mighty One was repaired and they continued their journey up the coast of the Pacific Ocean.

However, fortune was not on their side as, about a third of the way through Chile, The Mighty One traveled her last kilometer.

The pair were stranded for several days before deciding to continue on foot.

The pair planned on catching a boat to Easter Island, but there was little luck.

It was around this time that Che began to think about the struggle of the people of South America and his place in the world.

In those star-filled nights, Che slowly began to realize that the struggle of the people was his struggle, too.

Although not as outspoken as Che, Alberto came to many of the same conclusions as his friend.

Despite their troubles, the pair walked deeper into Chile, encountering the struggle of the people along the way.

As they approached a large mining operation, they came upon a young Chilean couple struggling to make ends meet.

The pair were heading to the mines to work in dangerous conditions because, as Communists, they were unable to find other work.

This was a profound moment for Che. Later, as he wrote to his mother, he said:

"By the light of the single candle...the contracted features of the worker gave off a mysterious and tragic air...the couple, frozen stiff in the desert night, hugging one another, was a live representation of the proletariat of any part of the world."

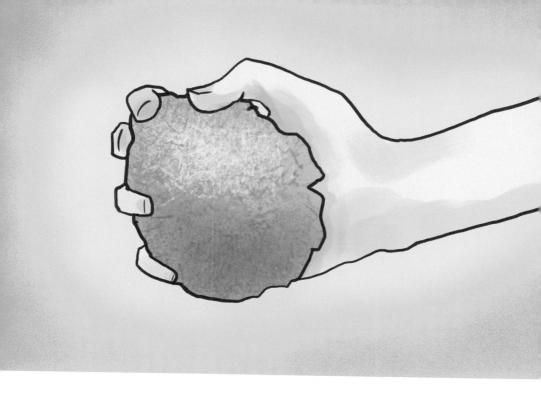

The next day, young Che would commit his first two acts of rebellion.

First, he attempted to hit the foreman of the Chilean mine, who was controlled by greedy businessmen, with a rock.

While his throw was errant, it was a sign of things to come.

A rebel streak had formed, ignited by the desire for a better world.

The second act, however, was less direct, but just as profound. Unknown to Alberto, Che had given all the money that Chichina had given him to the peasants.

Soon, Alberto and Che made their way to Peru. Without The Mighty One, they found themselves riding with workers in the back of a truck.

It was through this hitchhiking that the pair gained a greater understanding of the suffering of their people.

Once in Peru, the pair decided to hike their way up to the remains of the great Incan civilization, Machu Picchu.

As they hiked, they saw many locals. Che and Alberto took time to speak with them, learning of their sorrows and of their customs.

After a long hike, the pair finally reached Machu Picchu.

They could not help but find themselves in awe of the great ruin, built without the technology that the rest of the world said made their homeland primitive.

The pair spent several days at the site writing, debating, and, often, quietly contemplating.

It was here that their resolve grew, especially Che's. He began to see his homeland as one that was repressed, constantly held under the thumb of those who would seek to take advantage of it.

After leaving Machu Picchu, the pair spent some time speaking to the local native population.

In the course of these conversations, they grew angry at how the government and businesses treated the natives and admired the people's resilience and their desire to hold on to their heritage.

Their trip carried on, sometimes by foot, sometimes in the back of a truck, but always onward.

They spent several days in various areas of Peru, working as lecturers and treating Che's asthma.

Finally, they arrived in Lima, their last stop before they reached the leper colony.

It was here they met Dr. Hugo Pesce, the head of the leper colonies in Peru and a prominent Communist.

Che would later recount how Hugo had a profound effect on his life and how he viewed the world.

In fact, it was under Dr. Pesce's guidance that Che read Karl Marx for the first time.

It was a world-changing moment.

The two finally arrived at the leper colony. Several doctors showed them around and Che could not help but find disappointment in the fact that the patients were separated from their doctors by the mighty Amazon River.

He also took issue with how the nuns treated the patients, refusing to feed them if they did not attend Mass.

One of the first patients who Alberto and Che met at the colony was a young woman named Silvia.

She was a beautiful woman, despite leprosy, yet her illness had left her sullen and depressed.

While Alberto worked with the other patients in the colony to make their lives better, Che took an interest in Silvia.

He explained to her how his asthma made his life difficult and how she should keep fighting, to make her life better.

Despite some reluctance, Silvia agreed to keep fighting, and the pair got better together.

It was not all good news at the colony, however, as both Che and Alberto found themselves denied lunch on Sundays.

Che and Alberto stuck to their beliefs, however, willing to go hungry before they went to a Mass that they did not believe in.

Their patients, however, saw to it that they did not go hungry for long.

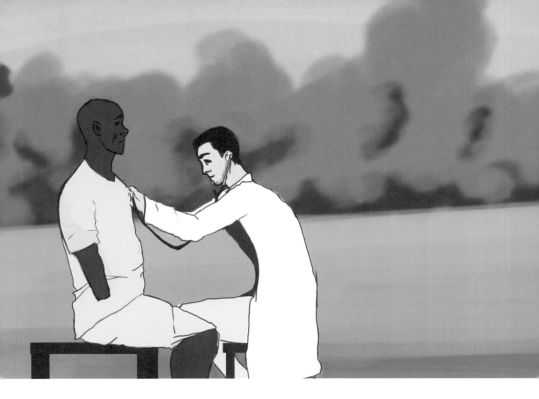

In spite of this, Alberto and Che were well received by their patients at the colony.

Not only did they treat their leprosy, but they also helped them build their homes, tend their animals, and plow their fields.

...and they even found time for some *futbol!*

After several weeks, time brought on Che's twenty-fourth birthday.

He was so adored by everyone at the colony, including the nuns, that they threw him a great party.

On the doctor's side of the river, they drank, and danced, and celebrated.

Emboldened by what they had experienced and what they had lived, Alberto encouraged Che to speak to the gathering on his newfound beliefs.

Rising for a toast, Che addressed the party, saying:

"And so, in an attempt to break free from all narrow-minded provincialism, I propose a toast to Peru and to a United America!"

A little later, Che stood on the banks of the mighty Amazon feeling lost.

This was the last night in the colony for him and Alberto, and as he drank and danced with his comrades, his patients sat, separated, on the other side of the river.

It was more than Che could stand.

Without a word to Alberto, Che began to swim the mighty river, full of piranhas and snakes, at night. It was a distance of more than two miles!

Alberto panicked, in part because of Che's asthma, but also because there was little he could do but watch.

Che was determined to spend his birthday with his patients!

He swam and swam, struggling against both the currents of the river and his own breathing…

…until he arrived, happy yet exhausted, into the arms of his patients.

Alberto, of course, knew all along that he'd make it.

The next day, Che and Alberto said goodbye to their friends, and to their patients, and

...to the nuns...

...to the doctors...

...to Silvia...

...and to everyone else in the colony.

The staff, who all thought fondly of the pair, gave them one more gift: a raft to float them upriver!

The two traveled on to Colombia, where, after a few more short stops, they parted company.

Alberto was taking a job back in Argentina and Che wanted to travel on to Venezuela and, perhaps, the United States.

The two friends hugged and parted ways, destined to see each other again only when they had changed the world...

And all because they had allowed the world to change them.

THE END

"Allow the world to change you, and you can change the world."

-Ernesto "Che" Guevara

ABOUT THE AUTHOR

M. Earl Smith is a historian, professor, author, and father. A graduate of Chatfield College in Ohio, he completed a master of arts degree in English at the University of Pennsylvania in 2017. He is currently pursuing a master of fine arts degree in creative writing at Pine Manor College while teaching English at Harcum College in nearby Bryn Mawr. He lives in Philadelphia with his Shetland Sheepdog, Che.

ABOUT THE ILLUSTRATOR

Gustavo Ferrés is a student of design at the College of Architecture and Urbanism at the University of São Paulo in Brazil. He is a native of São Paulo.

CPSIA information can be obtained
at www.ICGtesting.com
Printed in the USA
LVHW07n0129030918
588974LV00001B/5/P